MAKE ME THE BEST

BASEBALL PLAYER

BY TODD KORTEMEIER

SportsZone

An Imprint of Abdo Publishing
abdopublishing.com

abdopublishing.com

Published by Abdo Publishing, a division of ABDO, PO Box 398166, Minneapolis, Minnesota 55439. Copyright © 2017 by Abdo Consulting Group, Inc. International copyrights reserved in all countries. No part of this book may be reproduced in any form without written permission from the publisher. SportsZone™ is a trademark and logo of Abdo Publishing.

Printed in the United States of America, North Mankato, Minnesota
092016
012017

Cover Photos: Terry Jack/iStockphoto, top left; Nagel Photography/Shutterstock Images, top right; Action Sports Photography/Shutterstock Images, middle left; Shutterstock Images, bottom left; John Bazemore/AP Images, bottom right
Interior Photos: Terry Jack/iStockphoto, 4 (top); Action Sports Photography/Shutterstock Images, 4 (middle); Shutterstock Images, 4 (bottom); Nagel Photography/Shutterstock Images, 4–5 (top); John Bazemore/AP Images, 4–5 (bottom); Jeff Chiu/AP Images, 7; David Dennis/Icon Sportswire, 11; Gene J. Puskar/AP Images, 8, 13, 45; John Cordes/Icon Sportswire/AP Images, 15; Keith Gillett/Icon Sportswire/AP Images, 16; Erik Williams/Cal Sport Media/AP Images, 19; Gregory Bull/AP Images, 21; Ross D. Franklin/AP Images, 22; Mike Buscher/Cal Sport Media/AP Images, 25; Chris Williams/Icon Sportswire, 27; Marcio Jose Sanchez/AP Images, 29; Damon Tarver/Cal Sport Media/AP Images, 30; Matt Slocum/AP Images, 33; David Zalubowski/AP Images, 35, 36; Mark Goldman/Icon Sportswire/AP Images, 39; Gary Landers/AP Images, 41, 42

Editor: Patrick Donnelly
Series Designer: Nikki Farinella

Content Consultant: Parker Hageman, high school baseball coach, senior editor of TwinsDaily.com

Publisher's Cataloging-in-Publication Data

Names: Kortemeier, Todd, author.
Title: Make me the best baseball player / by Todd Kortemeier.
Description: Minneapolis, MN : Abdo Publishing, 2017. | Series: Make me the best athlete | Includes bibliographical references and index.
Identifiers: LCCN 2016945594 | ISBN 9781680784862 (lib. bdg.) | ISBN 9781680798142 (ebook)
Subjects: LCSH: Baseball--Juvenile literature.
Classification: DDC 796.357--dc23
LC record available at http://lccn.loc.gov/2016945594

TABLE OF

CONTENTS

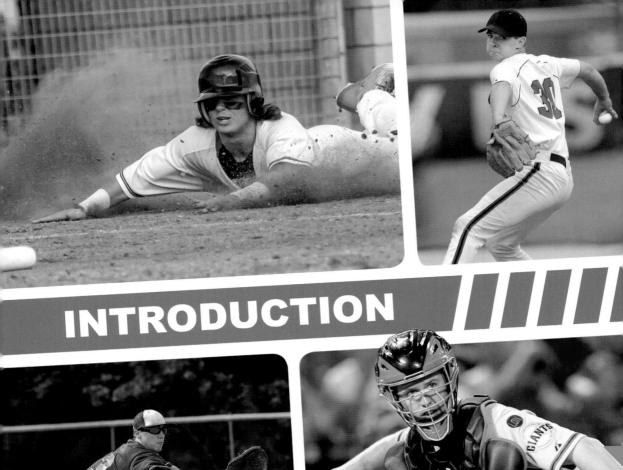

INTRODUCTION

The best baseball players in the world didn't become the best by accident. Being a great player takes a lot of hard work, some natural ability, and a little bit of luck. Every flamethrower or slugger started out as just another kid on the practice field. This book will show you how some of the best in the game got to where they are and how they maintain their all-star careers.

PITCH LIKE

CLAYTON KERSHAW

Facing Clayton Kershaw can make even the best hitters look like rookies. Kershaw's pinpoint control and blazing speed make his fastball a nightmare. His slider is hard with wicked movement. And his curveball starts at a batter's nose and ends at his knees. When Kershaw is on a roll, the only question is which pitch he will use to embarrass a hitter.

////////// **Kershaw won the 2012 Roberto Clemente Award for combining good play with service in the community.**

The Los Angeles Dodgers took Kershaw with the seventh overall pick in the 2006 Major League Baseball (MLB) draft. On May 25, 2008, at the age of 20, he made his major league debut. Kershaw struck out the side in the first inning. And he hasn't slowed down since. Kershaw won his first National League (NL) Cy Young Award,

Clayton Kershaw rears back to throw a pitch for the Los Angeles Dodgers.

which is given to the best pitcher in the league, at the age of 23. And at 26, he became the youngest pitcher in baseball history to win the award three times.

One of the keys to Kershaw's success is consistency. He likes to keep the same routine before each game. It helps him relax mentally and focus on other things. He follows a

PITCH LIKE CLAYTON KERSHAW

- To grip a four-seam fastball like Kershaw's, hold the ball with the seams facing you. The seams should look like a backward C if you are left-handed or a C if you are right-handed.

- Place the first knuckle of your index and middle fingers over the top seams.

- Set the ball back in your hand so the bottom seams are touching the spot where your index finger and middle finger join with your palm.

- Place your thumb on the seams on the bottom of the ball.

- Your ring finger should be curled with the middle knuckle pressed against the side of the ball for support. Your pinkie should not touch the ball.

Kershaw demonstrates his four-seam fastball grip.

strict warmup and practice schedule. In bullpen sessions between starts, he throws the same pattern of 34 pitches. Five hours before a game he starts, he throws softly against a wall. A little more than an hour before a game, he'll go over scouting reports with Dodgers coaches. These reports contain information about the opposing team's hitters. The reports tell Kershaw the batters' strengths and weaknesses.

Kershaw has five pitches he can throw during a game: four-seam fastball, curveball, slider, changeup, and sinker.

SANDY KOUFAX

Only two Dodgers have won three Cy Young Awards. The first was Sandy Koufax. He began his career with the Dodgers in 1955, when they played in Brooklyn, New York. Koufax and the Dodgers moved to Los Angeles in 1958, and he played the rest of his career there. Like Kershaw, Koufax was a left-hander. He threw four no-hitters in his career, including a perfect game in 1965. Injuries cut short his career after just 12 seasons. But he was still inducted into the National Baseball Hall of Fame in 1972.

During his windup, Kershaw hides the ball in his glove until the last possible moment.

That mix keeps hitters guessing. Kershaw's curveball is especially effective. It can drop up to 5 feet (1.5 m). The pitch keeps hitters hopelessly off-balance again and again.

Hitters try to identify a pitch as soon as possible to give them more time to decide whether to swing. But Kershaw hides the ball well. In his motion, the ball is hidden in his glove until very late. By the time the hitter can properly identify the pitch, it's usually too late to adjust.

Kershaw also pauses in the middle of his windup. That pause makes it hard for the hitter to time the pitch properly.

Kershaw won both the Cy Young and NL Most Valuable Player (MVP) Awards in 2014.

Kershaw's unique motion helps him deceive hitters. But that style wasn't intentional. It just felt comfortable and natural to him. Kershaw also studies video of opponents to understand their tendencies. But he never studies video of himself. Ever the perfectionist, Kershaw says he'll only see the flaws.

DRILL DOWN!

Here's a fun game that will help build up arm strength and accuracy.

1. You and a partner stand 30 feet apart and play catch.

2. When you're warmed up, begin aiming for three targets—your partner's face, torso, and beltline.

3. You score 3 points for a ball your partner catches in front of his face; the torso is worth 2; the beltline is worth 1.

4. The first player to score exactly 21 points wins. If you go over 21, your score goes back to 16.

PLAY OUTFIELD LIKE
LORENZO CAIN

Any time a hitter drives a ball deep into the gap, he's thinking he's got a sure double. Maybe even a triple. But not if Kansas City Royals center fielder Lorenzo Cain is on the job. Cain is famous for turning extra-base hits into outs.

Cain was a great athlete even as a boy. But basketball was his sport then. He didn't play baseball at all until his sophomore year in high school. After five years in the minors, Cain made it to the big leagues in 2010. By 2015, he was an all-star, an MVP candidate, and a World Series champion. He also is one of the best outfielders in baseball.

Cain uses his speed on the base paths, too. He stole 28 bases in 2015, the second most in the American League (AL).

Lorenzo Cain's fearless approach at the fence helps him make eye-popping defensive plays.

14

Cain's physical abilities help make him great. He's a fast runner with great leaping ability. That speed helps him cover a lot more ground than most other outfielders. He can track down almost any fly ball. But Cain is also a smart player. He works on his fielding while his teammates are taking batting practice. He pays attention to the sound of the ball coming off the bat and how far a fly ball carries.

PLAY OUTFIELD LIKE LORENZO CAIN

- Mind your depth. It's easier to go in on the ball than back on it, so you're usually better off playing deeper, especially for power hitters.

- Know the hitter. If he usually pulls the ball, take a few steps toward his pull side. If he likes to hit to the opposite field, shade him the other way.

- Watch the wind. Be aware of how it might affect the flight of the ball. If there's a flagpole at the ballpark, keep an eye on the flag to get an idea of how hard and which way the wind is blowing.

- Use your ears. The sound of the ball and bat meeting can give you an idea of how far the ball will carry.

Cain knows that communication is important when you're chasing a fly ball.

That helps him react immediately and get in position to make the catch.

Cain's knowledge also helps his teammates. He helps his fellow outfielders figure out where they should be positioned. And he calls out the location of fly balls and who should be in position to catch them. Cain also is fearless. He often risks injury to take a hit away from opponents. His daring play might make Royals fans nervous. But those risks are a big part of what makes him great.

Cain was named MVP of the 2014 AL Championship Series.

ANDRUW JONES

Andruw Jones was just 19 years old when he made his debut with the Atlanta Braves in 1996. He immediately was one of the best center fielders in the game. He won the Gold Glove Award in 10 straight seasons. Jones had incredible range and a strong arm. He had 10 or more assists from the outfield in seven seasons. He could track down almost any ball and could throw out almost any runner.

DRILL DOWN!

Practice taking the right angle on a fly ball with this drill.

1. Line up facing your partner about 20 feet away.

2. Have your partner point to the left or right. Cross your feet and run back at an angle in that direction, still watching your partner.

3. Your partner should throw a fly ball that you have to run hard to catch or a shorter fly ball that allows you to get into throwing position before making the catch.

4. Your partner can make you change directions before throwing. That simulates how the ball can move on a windy day.

HIT LIKE

MIKE TROUT

Mike Trout was born to be a ballplayer. But hard work made him a superstar.

Trout's father, Jeff, played four years in the minor league system of the Minnesota Twins. Jeff passed along his love of the game to his son. By the time he was eight years old, Mike was winning backyard Wiffle ball games against his dad. Mike turned pro straight out of high school. The Los Angeles Angels selected him late in the first round of the 2009 MLB Draft. He quickly became one of the top prospects in baseball.

Trout finished either first or second in MVP voting in each of his first four full major league seasons.

Trout was seen as a player who could do it all. He hit for average and for power, played outstanding defense, and

Mike Trout follows through after ripping a single in the 2016 All-Star Game.

ran the bases well. In his first year in the minors, he hit .352. His 2010 season was off the charts, too. He hit .341 and stole 56 bases. The next year, a month before his 20th birthday, Trout made his major league debut.

The honors piled up fast. He won the AL Rookie of the Year Award and made his first All-Star Game in 2012. He finished second in AL MVP voting in 2012 and 2013. The next year he led the AL in runs scored and runs batted in (RBI) and he was named the AL MVP.

HIT LIKE MIKE TROUT

- Do your homework. Find out whatever you can about the pitcher you're about to face.

- Anticipate pitches. If you're ahead in the count, look for a fastball. If you're behind in the count, expect an offspeed pitch.

- Stay back. Don't transfer your weight to your front foot too soon. Staying patient will give you more time to recognize the pitch.

- Pick a spot. Identify an area of the strike zone where you handle pitches well. If the count is 2–0 or 3–1, don't swing unless you get a fastball in your sweet spot.

Trout works on all parts of his swing during batting practice.

Trout accomplished all that with an unusual swing. Many power hitters need to extend their arms to drive a ball. But Trout keeps his arms close to his body when he swings. That helps him turn on inside pitches. He hits to all fields with power, and he mashes pitches in the lower third of the strike zone.

Trout relies on his legs to generate power. When he swings, he rotates his hips quickly. That movement lets his arms and shoulders fly through the zone like a whip.

You probably thought you'd seen the last of tees when you graduated from T-ball. But Trout likes to use a tee for drills. He focuses on driving his hips toward the ball, with

WILLIE MAYS

When Mike Trout was a top prospect, many people compared him to Willie Mays. The longtime New York/San Francisco Giants legend was another center fielder who could do it all. Mays won two MVP awards with the Giants and made 24 All-Star Games. When he retired in 1973, his 660 career home runs trailed only Babe Ruth and Hank Aaron. But Mays also hit .300 or higher in 10 seasons.

A simple leg kick helps Trout keep his weight back until the last moment.

his back knee moving toward his front ankle. Trout also practices a one-hand drill. He swings with just his top hand on the bat, near the top of the grip.

Trout also is a big believer in eating healthy. MLB players are always on the go. Maintaining good eating habits on the road can be difficult. Trout works hard at home and on the road to give his body the fuel it needs.

Trout was the All-Star Game MVP in 2014 and 2015.

DRILL DOWN!

Mike Trout uses batting tees to help improve his plate coverage.

1. Place a tee on the plate so that it is set up on the back and far side of the plate.

2. As you swing, focus on hitting the ball to the opposite field.

3. Move the tee to the front and inside part of the plate.

4. This time, focus on hitting the ball up the middle, rather than pulling it down the line.

5. Do two or three sets of 10 to 15 swings on each side.

CATCH LIKE

BUSTER POSEY

Madison Bumgarner was struggling. It was Game 1 of the 2014 World Series. The San Francisco Giants' ace had just walked the Kansas City Royals' Lorenzo Cain to load the bases in the third inning.

Giants catcher Buster Posey went to the mound for a chat. His 20-second visit calmed Bumgarner down. The Royals' Eric Hosmer tapped the next pitch to second base, ending the inning. The Giants went on to win the game and the series. It was their third World Series championship in five years. Posey was behind the plate for all of them.

////////// **While at Florida State, Posey once played all nine positions in a single game.**

Posey had never played catcher until he went to college at Florida State University. Soon he was a natural

Buster Posey's strong arm helps him shut down opposing base runners.

at the position. In college, coaches usually call pitches. Before long Posey was calling the game on his own. He was drafted fifth overall by the Giants in 2008 and made his MLB debut the next year. He won the NL Rookie of the Year Award in 2010 and the NL MVP Award in 2012.

Pitchers who have worked with Posey usually remark on his leadership. He stays calm, never panics, and keeps pitchers confident. Posey studies hitters and learns

CATCH LIKE BUSTER POSEY

- Get a grip. When throwing to a base, find the seams of the ball before you throw. It will improve your accuracy.

- Be subtle. Don't move your whole arm when you frame a pitch. A slight twist of the glove can sell a strike to the umpire.

- Move your feet. Don't rely on your glove to do the work on a pitch in the dirt. Shuffle your feet, hit your knees, and use your chest to block the ball.

- Use your head. Know what your pitcher likes to throw in different situations. Know what pitches the hitters are expecting.

Posey uses his chest to block pitches in the dirt whenever possible.

their tendencies. He excels at framing a pitch on the edge of the plate to get a strike call.

Posey also has become one of the best in baseball at throwing out runners. He regularly ranks among the leaders in caught-stealing percentage. Posey works on arm strength in the offseason. He also focuses on the angle of his hand to make sure he'll be accurate on a throw to second base.

Posey missed most of the 2011 season with a broken leg, but he came back the next year to win the NL batting title and MVP Award.

JOHNNY BENCH

When Johnny Bench made his debut in 1967, catchers were lucky to have one skill. Some could throw out runners. Some excelled at calling pitches. A few could hit. Bench could do all of that and more. The Cincinnati Reds star was a two-time NL MVP and won 10 Gold Gloves. Bench finished his career with 327 homers as a catcher, which is an all-time record. He also changed how catchers play the game. Bench was the first player to wear a helmet while catching. He also popularized the one-handed catching style that players use today.

DRILL DOWN!

Use this drill to perfect your pitch-blocking technique.

1. In full gear, squat behind the plate and have your partner kneel or sit 20 feet in front of you.

2. As your partner throws balls in the dirt, block them so that the ball stays in front of you. Deaden the ball by rolling your shoulders forward.

3. Scoop up the ball and get to your feet in throwing position.

4. Do 10 reps straight on, then 10 reps to your left and to your right.

PLAY INFIELD LIKE

NOLAN ARENADO

Colorado Rockies third baseman Nolan Arenado is a fan favorite. He hits the ball a mile, runs the bases well, and makes all the plays in the field. He even makes some plays that aren't on the field. Arenado has been known to dive into the seats at full speed while chasing a pop fly. He usually emerges from the crowd with the ball in his glove and a huge smile on his face.

////////// Arenado can hit, too. He led the NL in home runs and RBIs in 2015.

Arenado has good instincts at third base. And he has quick reflexes that help him react when the ball is hit. In 2013 he won a Gold Glove Award as a rookie, and he did it again in each of the next two years. He was an All-Star and an MVP candidate in 2015.

Nolan Arenado isn't afraid to go the extra mile to make a big catch.

Instincts are a big part of Arenado's game. But instincts go hand-in-hand with preparation. Arenado learns the tendencies of opposing hitters. He also works with his middle infielders, who can see the pitch their catcher is calling. A little signal of what's coming helps Arenado anticipate the play.

Arenado's brother Jonah is a player in the San Francisco Giants' minor league system.

PLAY INFIELD LIKE NOLAN ARENADO

- Know who's running. If the runner is slow, you will have more time to set yourself and make a strong throw.

- Take charge. On a slow roller in front of you, you won't have time to use your glove. Pick up the ball with your bare hand and throw to first in one motion.

- Get off your heels. As the pitch is delivered, keep your weight moving forward slightly or even take a small step forward. That will help you react to a ball hit to either side.

- On your toes! When chasing a pop fly, try to run on the balls of your feet as much as possible. That position will keep your head still and let you see the ball better.

Even when he's off-balance, Arenado makes sure to get his throw on target.

When fielding the ball, Arenado stays low and keeps his glove down. If the ball is hit to his right, he'll move his feet and try to get in front of the ball. If he can't get there in time, he catches the ball backhanded. He turns his body toward first, aligns his hips, and gets off a good throw.

But third basemen aren't always able to set their feet and make a proper throw. If he has to dive or charge a slow roller, the throw might be rushed and off-balance. Arenado still tries to square his shoulders to first base and make the throw as accurate as possible.

OZZIE SMITH

Ozzie Smith was known as "The Wizard." He didn't get the nickname just because of his first name. It was because of the magic he performed in the field. He was an acrobatic shortstop who could get to almost any ball. He could throw on the run or even from midair. Smith won 13 Gold Glove Awards in a 19-year career with the San Diego Padres and the St. Louis Cardinals. He considered himself an artist on the field. In every game, he tried to give fans something that they'd never seen before.

DRILL DOWN!

Develop soft hands with this classic exercise.

1. Attach a handle or knob to the back of a board about the size of your hand.

2. Put your bare glove hand through the handle so the flat surface takes the place of your palm.

3. Have a teammate or coach hit you ground balls.

4. Work on moving your hands back slightly as you trap the ball against the board with your bare hand. That will deaden the ball and keep it from bouncing away.

STEAL BASES LIKE

BILLY HAMILTON

Catchers know they have to keep an eye on Billy Hamilton. The Cincinnati Reds outfielder is one of the fastest players in baseball. And he's also a smart base runner. He can take advantage of any opportunity. He'll even steal a base on a routine throw back to the pitcher.

Hamilton was a multi-sport athlete in high school. He played baseball, basketball, and football. He was offered a football scholarship at Mississippi State University. But he decided to play baseball after the Reds drafted him in the second round in 2009. He soon showed off his blazing speed on the diamond.

Hamilton finished second in NL Rookie of the Year voting in 2014.

In 2011 Hamilton stole 103 bases in the low minor leagues. The next year, he set a minor league record

Billy Hamilton is one of baseball's top base stealers.

with 155 steals. He reached the major leagues in 2013. He finished second in the NL with 56 stolen bases in 2014 and 57 in 2015.

Hamilton certainly is fast. But there's more to stealing a base than just speed. Hamilton gets a great jump.

STEAL BASES LIKE BILLY HAMILTON

- Watch the pitcher's left heel. If a right-hander's left heel comes off the ground while the right one is still on the rubber, he's usually throwing home.

- The knee knows. If the back knee bends when the pitcher starts moving, he's likely throwing home.

- Keep an eye on lefties. If the right foot crosses the rubber after he lifts it, the pitcher has to throw home.

- Study habits. Pitchers are creatures of habit. Try to find a pattern in how many times he looks over at you before he throws home. Time how long he likes to hold the ball at the set position before he delivers the pitch.

Hamilton is so fast that catchers often don't bother throwing to second base to try to catch him.

He takes off at the first possible moment. Often the catcher doesn't even make a throw to second base.

One challenge to Hamilton's game is his reputation. Teams know he's fast. So pitchers try a variety of pickoff moves to keep him close to first base. Hamilton studies the pitcher's motion. He takes note of how quickly a pitcher gets the ball to the plate. If the pitcher delivers it quickly, Hamilton knows he'll need a bigger lead or a better jump.

As a high school freshman, Hamilton ran a 40-yard dash in 4.5 seconds. That's the same type of speed as an NFL running back.

RICKEY HENDERSON

Rickey Henderson loved the game of baseball. He did whatever he could to help his team win. Stealing bases was what he did best. Henderson stole a record 1,406 bases in his 24-year career. He led the league in steals 12 times, including a record 130 stolen bases in 1982. His superhuman speed earned him the nickname "The Man of Steal."

DRILL DOWN!

Improve reaction time and quickness with this fun exercise.

1. Start in a base-stealing stance with your partner about five yards to your right.

2. Your partner raises his hand holding a tennis ball. When he drops the ball, explode out of your stance and try to catch it.

3. If you catch it in the air, your partner should step back.

4. Make it a game by giving points for catching it in the air or on one or two bounces.

GLOSSARY

ASSIST

A play in which a fielder throws a runner out.

BULLPEN

The area where a team's pitchers warm up before and during a game.

CHANGEUP

A pitch that looks like a fastball but is thrown much slower to deceive the hitter.

DRAFT

The process by which teams select players who are new to the league.

MINOR LEAGUES

A lower level of baseball where players work on improving their skills before they reach the major leagues.

PERFECT GAME

A complete game in which the starting pitcher retires every batter, allowing no base runners.

PICKOFF

A play in which a player is tagged out before being able to get back to the base he is on.

ROOKIE

A first-year player.

TENDENCIES

How players usually perform.

WINDUP

A pitcher's throwing motion.

FOR MORE INFORMATION

BOOKS

Bryant, Howard. *Legends: The Best Players, Games, and Teams in Baseball*. New York: Philomel Books, 2015.

Hoblin, Paul. *Mike Trout: MLB Superstar*. Minneapolis, MN: Abdo Publishing, 2016.

Howell, Brian. *Baseball Trivia*. Minneapolis, MN: Abdo Publishing, 2016.

WEBSITES

To learn more about baseball, visit **booklinks.abdopublishing.com**. These links are routinely monitored and updated to provide the most current information available.

PLACE TO VISIT

National Baseball Hall of Fame and Museum
25 Main Street
Cooperstown, NY 13326
(888) 425-5633
www.baseballhall.org
Officially dedicated on June 12, 1939, the Hall of Fame and Museum draws approximately 300,000 people a year to the three-story facility that includes exhibits about people elected to the Hall of Fame, as well as memorabilia, photos, and multimedia presentations about the sport's history, issues, and personalities.

INDEX

ABOUT THE AUTHOR

Todd Kortemeier studied journalism and English at the University of Minnesota and has authored dozens of books for young people, primarily on sports topics. He lives in Minneapolis, Minnesota, with his wife.